Milk Carton MANIA

Christine M. Irvin

DISCARD

Children's Press®

A Division of Scholastic Inc.

New York • Toronto • London • Auckland • Sydney

Mexico City • New Delhi • Hong Kong

Danbury, Connecticut

The author and publisher are not responsible for injuries or accidents that occur during or from any craft projects. Craft projects should be conducted in the presence of or with the help of an adult. Any instructions of the craft projects that require the use of sharp or other unsafe items should be conducted by or with the help of an adult.

Design and Production by Function Thru Form Inc.
Illustrations by Mia Gomez, Function Thru Form Inc.
Photographs ©: School Tools/Joe Atlas

Library of Congress Cataloging-in-Publication Data

Irvin, Christine M.
      Milk carton mania / by Christine M. Irvin
         p. cm. — (Craft mania)
      ISBN 0-516-21673-2 (lib. bdg.)   0-516-27759-6 (pbk.)
      1. Box craft—Juvenile literature. 2. Milk containers—Juvenile literature.
      [1. Box craft. 2. Milk containers. 3. Handicraft.] I. Title. II. Series.

      TT870.5 .I775 2002
      745.5—dc21

                        00-046605

CHILDREN'S PRESS and associated logos are trademarks and or registered trademarks of Grolier Publishing Co., Inc.
SCHOLASTIC and associated logos are trademarks and or registered trademarks of Scholastic Inc.

1 2 3 4 5 6 7 8 9 10 R 11 10 09 08 07 06 05 04 03 02

Table of Contents

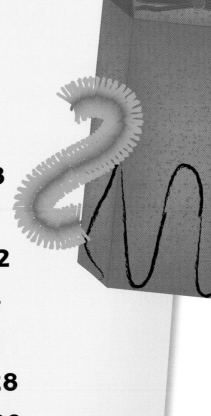

Welcome to the World
of Craft Mania 4

What You Will Need 6

Quick-and-Easy
Building Blocks 8

Perky Penguin 10

Space Shuttle 12

Carton Cat 14

Ring the Bell 16

Handy Basket 18

Kooky Clown 20

Happy House 22

Crazy Critter 24

Bird Feeder 26

Wishing Well 28

Castle Magic 30

Index 32

Welcome to the World of
CRAFT MANIA!

Don't throw away that milk carton! Everyday items, such as milk and juice cartons, cardboard tubes, paper cups, and paper plates, can become exciting works of art. You can have fun doing the projects and help save the environment at the same time by recycling these household objects instead of just throwing them away.

You can find ways to reuse many things around your home in craft projects. Bottle caps, buttons, old dried beans, and seeds can become eyes, ears, or a nose for an animal. Instead of buying construction paper, you can use scraps of wrapping paper or even last Sunday's comics to cover your art projects. Save the twist ties from bags of bread or vegetables—they make great legs! These are just a few examples of how you can turn trash into art. Try to think of other things in your home that can be used in your crafts.

 # Did You Know?

- Each person creates about 4 pounds (1.8 kilograms) of garbage per day.

- Each person in the United States uses about 580 pounds (260 kg) of paper every year. Businesses in the United States use enough paper to circle the earth 20 times every day!

- Americans use enough cardboard each year to make a paper bale as big as a football field.

- Americans throw away more than 60 billion food and drink cans (like tin cans and soft drink cans) and 28 billion glass bottles and jars (like those from ketchup and pickles) every year.

That's a lot of trash!

What you will need

It's easy to get started on your craft projects. The crafts in this book require some materials you can find around your home, some basic art supplies, and your imagination.

Buttons, bottle caps, beads, old dried beans, or seeds for decoration

Glue

Tape

Tempera paints

Colored markers

Hole puncher

Construction paper (or newspaper or scraps of wrapping paper)

Felt (or scraps of fabric)

Twist ties (or pipe cleaners)

You might want to keep your craft materials in a box so that they will be ready any time you want to start a craft project. Now that you know what you need, look through the book and pick a project to try. Become a Craft Maniac!

A Note to Grown-Ups

Older children will be able to do most of the projects by themselves. Younger ones will need more adult supervision. All of them will enjoy making the items and playing with their finished creations. The directions for most of the crafts in this book require the use of scissors. Do not allow young children to use scissors without adult supervision.

☞ Helpful Hints

Remember to rinse out the cartons and let them dry before beginning any project. Poking holes in milk cartons can be challenging so make sure to ask a grown-up for help if you have trouble. When gluing items onto milk cartons, it helps to use big rubber bands to hold things in place while the project dries. Bag clips or big binder clips can be used to keep a milk carton closed while waiting for the glue to dry.

Quick-and-Easy Building Blocks

What you need

- **Two milk cartons, the same size, for each building block**

- **Scissors** (Before cutting any material, please ask an adult for help.)

What you do

1 Have an adult help you cut the tops off both milk cartons.

2 Put one milk carton inside the other milk carton to make a solid block. Slide the open end of one carton inside the open end of the other carton, as shown. Squash the top of one carton a little to make it fit inside the other. Push the cartons together until one is completely inside the other.

Your building block is ready to use!

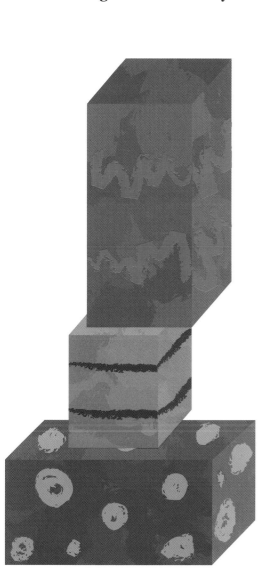

Other Ideas

○ Paint your block with tempera paints. Make sure the paint is completely dry before using the block.

○ Wrap your blocks in brown paper from an old grocery bag.

○ Build with these blocks. They make great forts and cool castles.

Perky Penguin

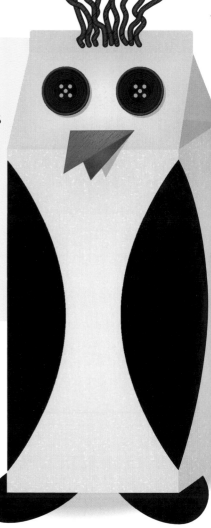

What you need

- One milk carton, any size
- One large white paper shopping bag, opened up to lie flat, or white construction paper
- Ruler
- Pencil
- Scissors (Before cutting any material, please ask an adult for help.)
- Glue
- Two big, black buttons
- Scrap of red felt
- Black yarn
- Scraps of black felt

What you do

1 Open up the top of the milk carton.

2 Cover the milk carton with the paper. Measure and mark the shopping bag so that it is big enough to cover the open carton from top to bottom, and around all four sides, with an extra ½-inch overlap all around. Have an adult help you cut the white paper. Spread a thin layer of glue around the whole carton. Apply paper to the carton. Use a small amount of glue to hold overlaps in place on the side and bottom.

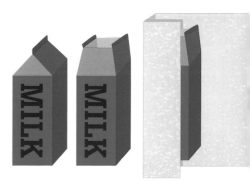

3 Close the carton top and glue shut.

4 Add eyes. Glue on the buttons for eyes.

5 Make the beak. Using the red felt, have an adult help you cut out a diamond shape for the beak, as shown. Fold the felt shape in half. Glue it in place on the penguin's face.

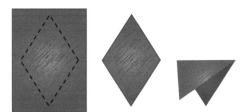

6 Add feathers. Glue scraps of black yarn to the top of the penguin's head. Let the glue dry.

7 Add the wings. Using black felt, have an adult help you cut out two wing shapes, as shown. The wings should be long enough to go from the top to the bottom of the penguin's body. Then, glue the wings in place. Let the glue dry.

8 Add the feet. Using black felt, have an adult help you cut out two feet shapes, as shown. Glue the feet in place on the bottom of the penguin's body. Let the glue dry.

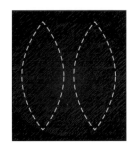

Other Ideas

○ Paint your penguin instead of covering the milk carton with paper.

○ Make a pair of bookends by making two penguins. Before you close the tops of the milk cartons in Step 3, fill each carton halfway with sand.

Space Shuttle

What you need

- One half-gallon milk carton
- One large white paper shopping bag, opened up to lie flat, or white construction paper
- Ruler
- Black marker
- Scissors (Before cutting any material, please ask an adult for help.)
- Glue
- Two soup cans or frozen orange juice cans
- Aluminum foil
- Four small, empty thread spools, all the same size or one cardboard tube cut into four 1½-inch sections

What you do

1. Open up the top of the milk carton.

2. Cover the milk carton. Measure and mark the white bag so that it is big enough to cover the open carton from top to bottom, and around all four sides, with an extra ½-inch overlap all around. Have an adult help you cut the paper. Spread a thin layer of glue around the whole carton. Apply paper to the carton. Use a small amount of glue to hold overlaps in place on the side and bottom.

3 Close the carton top and glue shut. Let the glue dry.

4 Cover the soup cans. Measure and mark a piece of aluminum foil so that it is big enough to cover one soup can from top to bottom, with an extra ½-inch overlap at the top. You will need a piece of foil about 8 inches by 8 inches. Have an adult help you cut the foil. Then, wrap the foil around the soup can, as shown. Fold down the edges of the foil at the top and bottom of the can to hold it in place. Cover the other soup can the same way.

5 Put your space shuttle together. Turn the soup cans upside-down. Spread a thick layer of glue on one side of one soup can.

Press the soup can in place on one side of the milk carton, as shown. Do the same thing with the other soup can. Let the glue dry.

6 Add exhaust pipes. Glue the four thread spools to the bottom of your space shuttle, as shown. Let the glue dry.

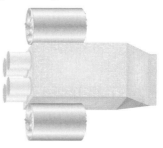

7 Add windows. Using the marker, draw in window shapes on your space shuttle anywhere you want them. Color them in with markers.

Other Ideas

○ Decorate your space shuttle with decals left over from model-building projects or with stickers.

○ Draw your own signs on your space shuttle with markers.

Carton Cat

What you need

- One milk carton, any size
- One large brown paper bag, opened up to lie flat
- Ruler
- Black marker
- Scissors (Before cutting any material, please ask an adult for help.)
- Glue
- Scraps of felt
- Three buttons
- Three twist ties or pipe cleaners
- One thick, fuzzy pipe cleaner or a scrap of furry material
- One bag clip or large binder clip

What you do

 Open up the top of the milk carton.

 Cover the milk carton with paper. Measure and mark the paper bag so that it is big enough to cover the open carton from top to bottom, and around all four sides, with an extra ½-inch overlap all around. Have an adult help you cut the brown paper. Spread a thin layer of glue around the whole carton. Apply paper to the carton. Use a small amount of glue to hold overlaps in place on the side and bottom.

3 Close the carton top and glue shut. Use a bag clip or large binder clip to hold the carton shut. Let the glue dry before going on to Step 4.

4 Add ears. Draw ear shapes on the felt, as shown. Have an adult help you cut them out. Glue them in place on the milk carton.

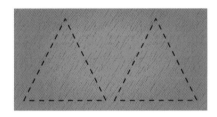

5 Add eyes. Glue the two buttons for eyes and one button for the nose.

6 Add whiskers. Glue the three twist ties on the face for whiskers. Let the glue dry before going on to Step 7.

7 Add the legs. Using the black marker, draw in legs for your cat.

8 Add a tail. Glue the thick, fuzzy pipe cleaner or the scrap of furry material in place, for the tail, as shown. Let the glue dry before playing with your cat.

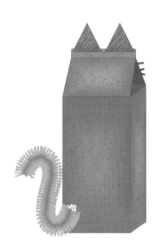

Other Ideas

○ Paint your cat. Instead of covering the milk carton with brown paper, paint it with tempera paints, using any colors you wish.

○ Turn your cat into a doorstop. Before you close the top of the milk carton in Step 3, fill the carton halfway with sand. This will make the carton heavy enough to hold a door open. Follow the rest of the directions to finish your cat.

Ring The Bell

What you need

- One half-gallon milk carton
- Scissors (Before cutting any material, please ask an adult for help.)
- Ruler
- Markers
- Construction paper
- Glue
- One piece of string, ribbon, or yarn about 18 inches long
- Two ½-inch bells
- Pen

What you do

1 Cut the top part off of a milk carton. Measure and draw a line 4 inches up from the bottom of the carton around all four sides. Have an adult help you cut along the line. The bottom part of the carton will be used for the bell.

2 Cover the bottom piece of the carton. On construction paper, trace around one side of the bell four times. Trace around the top one time. Have an adult help you cut out the pieces of paper. Spread a thin layer of glue on one side of the bell. Press a piece of construction paper onto the bell, keeping edges even. Glue on one piece of paper at a time until all four sides and top of the bell are covered. Let glue dry before going on to Step 3.

3 Add a hole to the carton. With an adult's help, use the pen to punch a hole in the middle of the top of the carton.

4 Make a clapper for the inside of the carton. The clapper is the part of the bell that hits the side and makes it ring. Have an adult help you cut a piece of ribbon or yarn 18 inches long. Fold the string in half and pull the looped end through the opening in the carton so that the string extends 4½ inches above the carton. Tie a knot above the carton and one below. Tie a bell to each end of the string inside the carton.

5 Decorate the carton. Use markers and draw designs on your bell.

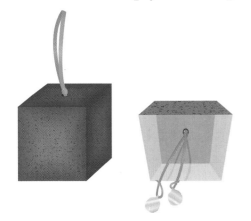

Other Ideas

- Paint your bell with tempera paints. Make sure the paint is completely dry before using the bell.

- Make an assortment of bells, using different sized milk cartons. Use a different sized bell for each clapper, a small one for small bells and larger ones for large bells.

- Cover your bell with wrapping paper for special events, such as birthdays and holidays.

Handy Basket

What you need

- One half-gallon milk carton
- Scissors (Before cutting any material, please ask an adult for help.)
- Glue
- Ruler
- Masking tape
- Pen
- Two paper fasteners
- Tempera paints
- Paintbrush

What you do

1 Open the top of the milk carton and have an adult help you cut one side off of the milk carton, as shown.

2 Close the end of the milk carton. Fold the remaining top flaps down and glue them together, as shown.

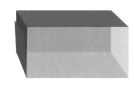

3 Make the handle. Measure and mark a 1-inch by 7½-inch piece from the side of the carton that you cut out in Step 1. Have an adult help you cut out the handle. Also, using a pen, punch a hole in each end of the handle, and two holes (one on each of the long sides of the basket) where you want the handles attached.

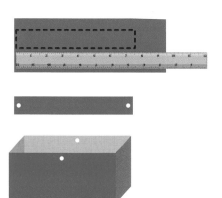

4 Attach the handle to the basket. Line up the holes in the handle with the holes in the basket. Slide a paper fastener through each hole, from the outside to the inside. Open the fasteners to hold the handle in place.

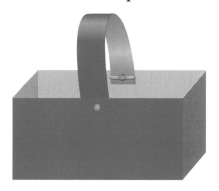

5 Paint your basket with tempera paints. Make sure the paint is completely dry before using your basket.

Other Ideas

- Cover the milk carton in construction paper instead of painting it.

- Use the basket as a planter. Place some pebbles in the bottom of the basket. Fill the basket with soil and plant a few seeds in the dirt. Water and watch your favorite plants grow.

- Use as a gift basket. After decorating your basket, fill it with small presents for a friend or member of your family.

Kooky Clown

What you need

- One half-gallon milk carton
- Glue
- Construction paper
- Ruler
- Scissors (Before cutting any material, please ask an adult for help.)
- One egg carton
- Two buttons
- Markers
- Cotton balls or scraps of yarn (for hair)
- One bag clip or large binder clip

What you do

1 Cover the milk carton with construction paper. Measure and mark a piece of construction paper big enough to cover one open carton from top to bottom, and around all four sides, with an extra ½-inch overlap all around. Have an adult help you cut the construction paper. Spread a thin layer of glue around the carton. Apply paper to the carton.

Smooth out wrinkles and overlap at top, bottom, and on each side as you go around. Use a small amount of glue to hold overlaps in place on the sides and bottom.

2 Glue the top of the milk carton together so it won't come open. Use a bag clip or large binder clip to hold the carton closed while the glue dries.

3 Have an adult help you cut the bottom half of an egg carton into three parts, as shown, each with two rows of two cups.

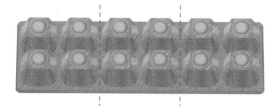

4 Glue one section of the egg carton on the bottom of your carton for legs. Glue one section on each side of the carton for arms.

5 Glue on buttons for eyes.

6 With markers, design a face for your clown.

7 Give your clown some hair by gluing on cotton balls or scraps of yarn. Let the glue dry before playing with your clown.

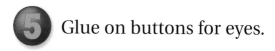

Other Ideas

- Decorate your clown's costume with fabric or paper in different designs.

- Add hands and shoes made from scraps of cardboard.

- Make a clown hat from construction paper or newspaper.

- Have a contest with your friends to see who can make the funniest or silliest clowns.

What you need

- One half-gallon milk carton
- One large brown paper bag, opened up to lie flat
- Ruler
- Markers

- Scissors (Before cutting any material, please ask an adult for help.)
- Glue
- One bag clip or large binder clip

What you do

 1 Open up the top of the milk carton.

2 Cover the milk carton. Measure and mark the paper bag so that it is big enough to cover the open carton from top to bottom, and around all four sides, with an extra ½-inch overlap all around. Have an adult help you cut the brown paper. Spread a thin layer of glue around the whole carton. Apply paper to the carton. Use a small amount of glue to hold overlapping pieces in place on the side and bottom.

3 Close the carton top and glue shut. Use a bag clip or large binder clip to hold the carton closed while the glue dries. Let glue dry before going on to Step 4.

4 Cut the carton into two sections. Draw a line around three sides of the milk carton with a marker about 3 inches from the bottom of the carton. Have an adult help you cut along the line. Then, fold the bottom part of the carton up and out. The big part of the carton will be the house and the small part will be the garage.

5 Attach the smaller part of the carton to the larger part. Spread a thick layer of glue on the side of the smaller part that touches the larger part, as shown. Use a bag clip or large binder clip to keep the house

and garage attached until the glue dries. Let the glue dry before going on to Step 6.

6 Add the doors. Using markers, draw a door shape on the house and a door shape on the garage.

7 Add windows. Using markers, draw window shapes on the house and the garage where you want them. Color in the window shapes with a marker.

Other Ideas

- Open the doors using scissors. Ask an adult for help cutting the doors.

- Color your house and garage with crayons.

- Paint your house and garage. Instead of covering the milk carton with brown paper, paint it with tempera paints, using any colors you wish.

- Make a town by building lots of houses.

Crazy Critter

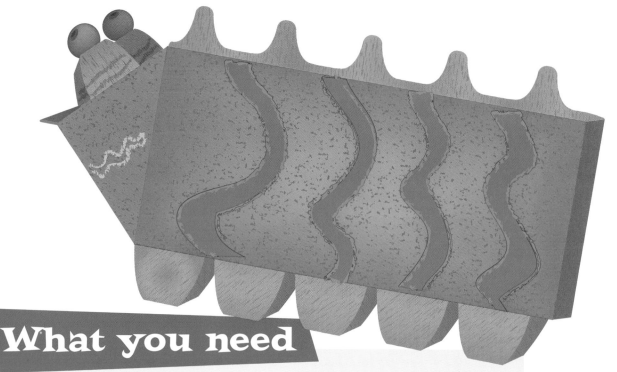

What you need

- One half-gallon milk carton
- One egg carton
- Tempera paints
- Paintbrush
- Glue
- Scissors (Before cutting any material, please ask an adult for help.)

What you do

1 Take the bottom of the egg carton and cut off one row of egg holders, as shown. Have an adult help you cut the carton.

2 Glue the larger section of the egg carton bottom to one side of the milk carton.

3 With the milk carton on its side, glue the two egg sections to one side of the peak of the carton's top. These two egg holders will be the critter's eyes. If the carton has a plastic spout at the top, glue the egg section to the side opposite the spout.

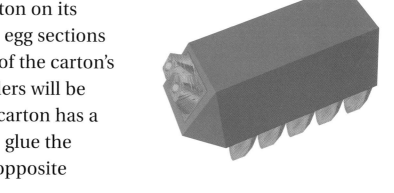

4 Take the top of the carton and cut off the edges, as shown. Glue the ridges from the top of the egg carton to the top of the milk carton.

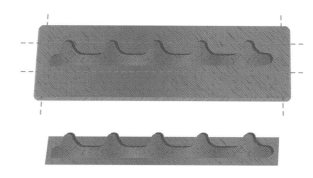

5 After the glue has dried, paint the egg holders and milk carton any colors you would like.

6 Add eyes and mouth with tempera paints. Let the paint dry before playing with your critter.

Other Ideas

○ Use buttons, beads, or seeds for your critter's eyes and mouth.

○ Make a rock monster by gluing on pebbles instead of painting your critter.

Bird Feeder

What you need

- One half-gallon milk carton
- Marker
- Scissors (Before cutting any material, please ask an adult for help.)
- Pen
- Two polystyrene plates
- One long piece of thick string
- Stick for perch

What you do

1 Make the square-shaped holes on the carton. Using the marker, draw squares in the front and the back of the carton, as shown. Have an adult help you cut out the shapes.

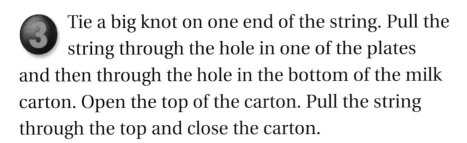

2 Make a hole in the center of each plate and in the bottom of the milk carton.

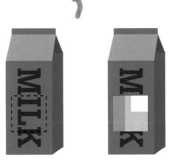

3 Tie a big knot on one end of the string. Pull the string through the hole in one of the plates and then through the hole in the bottom of the milk carton. Open the top of the carton. Pull the string through the top and close the carton.

4 Pull the string through the hole in the other plate.

5 Tie the end of the string at the top into a handle.

6 Add the perch. Using the pen, have an adult help you punch two holes in the feeder, one below each square opening. Push one end of the stick in through one hole and out through the other hole, as shown. Make sure the stick hangs out about the same amount on each side of your bird feeder.

7 Hang your bird feeder from a tree branch where birds can find it and other animals cannot reach it. Fill your feeder with sunflower seeds or other wild bird food.

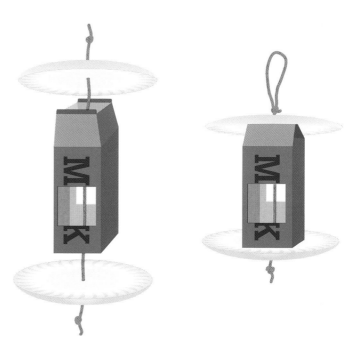

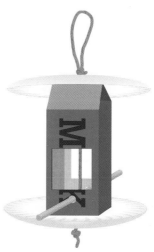

Other Ideas

- Get a book on birds out of the library and see if you can identify the types of birds that visit your feeder.
- Decorate your bird feeder.

Wishing Well

What you need

- One milk carton, any size
- Ruler
- Marker
- Scissors (Before cutting any material, please ask an adult for help.)
- Construction paper
- Glue
- Four craft sticks
- Lightweight cardboard

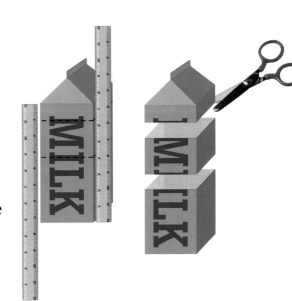

What you do

1 Cut the top part off of a milk carton. Draw a line about 1 inch from the top of the carton. Have an adult help you cut off the top of the carton along the line.

2 Make the base for the well. Measure and mark a line 4 inches up from the bottom of the carton around all four sides of the carton.

3. On a piece of construction paper, trace around one side of the carton base four times. Have an adult help you cut out the pieces of paper. Spread a thin layer of glue on one side of the wishing well. Press a piece of construction paper onto the well, keeping the edges even. Glue one piece of paper at a time until all four sides of the well are covered. Let the glue dry before going on to Step 4.

4. Lie the base on its side. Glue one craft stick flat against one of the inside corners of the well 1 inch down inside the carton. Let glue dry. Add the remaining craft sticks in each corner one at a time, as shown. Let the glue dry before going on to Step 5.

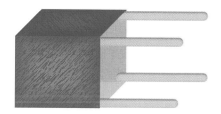

5. Make a roof for your well. Glue the four craft sticks inside each corner of the carton's top.

6. Finish the roof. Have an adult help you cut a piece of light-weight cardboard and a piece of construction paper the same size. Both pieces have to be big enough to cover the top of the milk carton. Glue the construction paper to the cardboard. Let the glue dry before going on to Step 7.

7. Fold the cardboard in half with the construction paper on the outside. Glue the cardboard to the top of the well.

Other Ideas

- Use scraps of fabric, wrapping paper, or newspaper to decorate the roof of your well.

- Glue pebbles around the base to make a stone well.

Castle Magic

What you need

- **Four milk cartons**
- **One cardboard box, roughly same height as milk cartons**
- **Construction paper**
- **Ruler**
- **Markers**
- **Scissors** (Before cutting any material, please ask an adult for help.)
- **Glue**
- **Toothpicks**
- **Four small beads**

What you do

1 Open up the top of the milk carton.

2 Cover the carton towers. Measure and mark a piece of construction paper big enough to cover one open carton from top to bottom, and around all four sides,

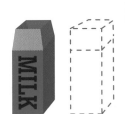 

30

with an extra ½-inch overlap all around. Have an adult help you cut the construction paper. Spread a thin layer of glue around the carton. Apply paper to the carton. Smooth out wrinkles and overlap at top, bottom, and on one side as you go around. Use a small amount of glue to hold overlaps in place on the side and bottom. Repeat the process for all carton towers.

3 Close each carton top and glue shut. Before the glue dries, insert a toothpick into the peak of each milk carton. Let glue dry before going on to Step 4.

4 Cover the cardboard box with construction paper. Make sure to overlap the paper at the top, bottom, and on one side of the box. Let glue dry before going on to Step 5.

5 Glue the carton towers to the outside of the box. Let glue dry before going on to Step 6.

6 Decorate your castle. Use markers to draw windows and a door on the castle towers.

7 Add flags. Glue small pieces of construction paper to toothpicks to make banners. Glue a small bead on the top of each toothpick to cover the end. Let glue dry before playing with your castle.

Other Ideas

- Add a drawbridge to the castle. Use a marker to draw an arched doorway in the front of the box, as shown. Have an adult help you cut out the shape (on both sides and the top), leaving the drawbridge attached to the box at the bottom. Fold drawbridge out.

- Cover your castle with newspaper or brown paper bags instead of construction paper.

Index

Basket, 18–19
Bell, 16–17
Bird feeder, 26–27
Blocks, 8–9

Castle, 30–31
Cat, 14–15
Clown, 20–21
Critter, 24–25

Helpful hints, 7
House, 22–23

Penguin, 10–11

Recycling, 4–5

Space shuttle, 12–13
Supplies, 6

Well, wishing, 28–29
Wishing well, 28–29

About the Author

Christine M. Irvin lives in the Columbus, Ohio area with her husband, her three children, and her dog. She enjoys writing, reading, doing arts and crafts, and shopping.